My Body Is Not an Apology

poems by

Megha Sood

Finishing Line Press
Georgetown, Kentucky

My Body Is Not an Apology

For my mother and father,
To whom I owe everything

ACKNOWLEDGMENTS

My gratitude goes to the editors of the following journals, in which these poems
originally appeared, sometimes in their earlier versions:

War Cry against the Uterus ~ "False ownership"
Whisper and the Roar ~ "My Body Is Not an Apology," "When Men Explain Me
Things," "An Exercise in Futility," "How To Be a Woman?"
Madness Muse Press ~ "Unappreciated," "Freedom, an Interpretation"
MookyChick ~ "Even My Grief Should Be Productive"
Headline Poetry ~ "resistance"
DOVE Tales, Writing for Peace Anthology ~ "Unforgivable"
Praxis Magazine ~ "Demarcation"
THE POET: War and Battle, Spring Edition ~ "Missed Boat"
Subterranean Blue Poetry ~ "An Act of Self Defense"
Culture Cult Anthology 2020, "My Body Lives Like a Continuous Threat"
Poetry Diversified 2020, National Level Winner of the Spring Robinson Lit Prize 2020
"Peace—A Metaphor for Denial"
She Speaks Up, The Jessie Butler Women's Poetry Contest Anthology 2020 ~ "Path to
My Freedom"
Winner of the State Level NAMI NJ Dara Axelrod Poetry Contest 2020 ~ "My
Survival Story"

I'm beyond grateful for the advice and support from my friends, family, and editors
for bringing this chapbook to fruition. My eternal gratitude goes to all the advance
readers of my chapbook for believing in my work and encouraging me every step of
the way. To my editor, Christen Kincaid, and all the folks at Finishing Line Press who
made my dream come true. And to my husband and my son whose love and strength
have kept me going against all odds.

Publisher: Leah Huete de Maines
Editor: Christen Kincaid
Cover Art: Mika Baumeister via Unsplash.com
Author Photo: Megha Sood
Cover Design: Elizabeth Maines McCleavy

Order online: www.finishinglinepress.com
also available on amazon.com

Author inquiries and mail orders:
Finishing Line Press
PO Box 1626
Georgetown, Kentucky 40324
USA

Table of Contents

Foreword of My Body Is Not An Apology, Megha Sood
by Candice Daquin

When I began reading Megha Sood several years ago, people talked about her prodigious work ethic, but what struck me viscerally was the truth of her writing. Writers disguise themselves in words. Sood dismisses that technique and puts herself front and center as a poet. Sood is a thinker, she's not a meme, she's a woman, she's larger than life, she's unapologetically asking you to think.

With such a plethora of competing voices, how does one distinguish oneself? Sood's approach works. She puts in a huge amount of effort and she's got the talent to back it up. Her work doesn't ever let you know, it always forces you to deeply consider and she's not going to give you an easy way out.

Whether you know it or not, poetry isn't meant to just lie softly in your mouth. It's meant to burn; it's meant to provoke a response. Poetry speaks to a generation, it's the antithesis of being quiet and well behaved. Sood follows a long tradition of women who speak out, and she does it as an Indian-American woman of great substance and depth.

Her greatest gift is this purity of intention; the way she truly feels is expressed succinctly on the page. Sood doesn't want you to enjoy reading her poetry, she wants you to consider what she's saying and question your assumptions.

It is no small thing to write in a language different from your language of origin. It isn't simply the language itself, it's the nuance. It takes years to master nuance. Some native speakers never accomplish this! So, for one who adopts a language and culture, it's even more impressive. Ironically it is often one coming into a culture, who can speak to that culture with the greatest alacrity and purpose. Maybe because they know what it feels like to look in from the outside.

Sood has titanic power in her elemental wielding of words. She has a precision most copywriters would die for, an editor's eye and a surging passionate heart filled with purpose. This ambition coupled with talent raises her game considerably and it is no surprise at all she has already carved a place for herself in the pantheon of modern poets.

Are you surprised a chapbook called *My Body Is Not an Apology* would be accepted by a leading publisher of poetry? It's a superb title, speaking to one of Sood's most invested beliefs; feminism and equality. Not only has Sood directly experienced discrimination but she's harnessed the rage of this experience into a well-honed tool; that of a female poet speaking her piece.

The collection is everything you'd imagine with such a powerhouse title, Sood doesn't let you down for a moment, her momentum is consistent and highly sculpted with the unforgettable words that are impossible to mislay:

"*The slow cleaving in my backbone*
the seamless transformation:
branching into my thousand selves
Like a sapling breaking
from the blind seed
I'm sprouting, I am thriving. " (My Survival Story)

One might argue, don't we switch off after a time, when we've read many empowerment books? That's like saying will we get fed-up of seeking equality for our gender? When a cause has an unending purpose and value, there is no tedium factor and it would take a lifetime of publishing to equalize the gender gap. So often we get co-opted into feeling sorry for the other side, without realizing true equality seeks no sides, and only asks for equal treatment. Sood doesn't hate men, she values herself as a woman and doesn't apologize for any aspect of it. If only we could all take a leaf out of her book.

Gender may no longer be as immutable as it was once considered, but gender inequality is still alive and kicking, from unequal pay, small or nonexistent maternity rights, women being shelved at a much younger age than men in the matchmaking market, or made invisible by age, disability, reproduction, income, and other inequities. It is not sufficient to make small progress, or pat ourselves on the back for a change. As long as Presidents who ridicule women can be elected into office, as long as #metoo movements are queried or derided, women must continue to fight for true equality. That includes within their own gender. Books like *My Body Is Not an Apology* aren't just necessary, they're the very fabric upon which we build a better future.

Women of color have had less access to this writing legacy than others, and all women have been restricted in their written histories. The value of passing down women's thinking is immeasurable. Each generation takes the learning from the past and interprets it for their own. The minute we stop doing this is the first step backward. Women's inner voices must never again be infused with shame or shut down by those who give them no value.

"*So next time the world tries to*
teach me how to be a woman
/an epitome of grace and elegance/

they should come and witness the scars
I bore on my body." (How To Be a Woman?)

I am excited to read these interpretations from women throughout the world, a myriad of cultures, experiences, and how their rich tapestry adds to, strengthens, the pre-existing movement. It would not be sufficient to have one canon. It would not be enough to have one ideology. So long as we all believe in the intrinsic truth of egality and equality, then our differences should be celebrated and we should not fall into the old trope ways of creating a narrow canon. Sood and her voice take us out of the white privilege and lend an enduring depth and modernity to the themes within feminism.

If you find unapologetic truth hard to read, you may struggle, but you should persevere. There is unending worth in truth, and Sood has her finger firmly pressed on the life pulse of all of us. Sood is
a writer who writes things other writers wish they had written. She's one of those writers who can say what we've been thinking before we have said it. Her voice is strong, uncompromising and thoughtful.

"Does scream have a religion too? Do cries have a race?
Does hurt have a gender? Do wounds have a nationality?" (Does Hurt Have A
Gender?)

I value the truth sayers of every epoch, I gravitate toward poets who put themselves out there and don't hold back. It is not an easy thing to do, it's a necessary thing to do, and Sood's reputation as an ethical, talented poet, is only going to increase with every step she takes toward setting us all free.

—Candice Louisa Daquin, Senior Editor, Indie Blu(e) Publishing

False Ownership

This is strangely annoying.
when you see arrogance in
someone who doesn't own a thing
can't conjure a thing out of thin air
let alone a human being.

You are just the renter here. You don't own shit.
you are born from this womb
that cradles your existence for months
a sliver away from called a being

Nothing but a pulsating existence in a foreign body
Sometimes the body treats it like an infection
to keep away the contamination
self-purging, an act of reclamation

Sometimes it accepts
cups its own palm
supports you, carries it to term
Its the body
the arrangement,
the unsaid understanding
a solemn promise;
between the body and its identity

Your existence is slowly molded
like a ball of sagging clay on the potter wheel
morphed and molded
to be called a human being

You don't own the womb.
You definitely don't own our bodies.
You break the arrangement
just like to possess the things

Let me clear this,
for the sake of your understanding
the body is not for your taking
There is a thin line between
The choices we make and your wanting.

My Body Is Not an Apology

This body—
My body is not an apology
It's a prayer.
Forgiveness wrapped in the filigrees end of my skin
frayed at the ends;
battered for so long
by your pointy convictions
and cookie-cutter rules which try
to shape and mold this body along.

My body is not an apology
it doesn't desire to fit in a frame
mapped inch by inch
else to be ashamed.

My body is not an apology
it's a roar: a declaration
an unapologetic,
unabashed
straight truth in your face
a war cry:
a deafening scream from the silence.

My body is not an apology
this body will not be mapped
as a benchmark for beauty,
an attempt to hide the crows-feet
or the spider veins
from your vile eyes
and your forked tongue.

My body is not an apology
but a safe haven
an epitome of affection,
a metaphor for crimson love
that flows in my veins for years to come.

My body is not an apology
It's an eye of the storm
a dance of destruction,
A safe haven for life

forgiveness in disguise.

With love neatly folded in the wrinkles of my skin
warmth oozing from every pore of my being
a lesson etched in every single crow's feet
forgiveness written through every inch of my spider veins

This body is not an apology—
But a profound lesson
a triumphant proclamation;
An unfettered declaration.

When Men Explain Me Things

The sharp wind
grazes and cuts my tongue
/razor-sharp/
like your disagreement towards
how I live my life
your pointy misconceptions
about how it has been traded for various things
to give you little pleasures
at the expense of my happiness

the black metallic taste
of my unspoken truths
sits at the back of my throat
mulling in obsidian time
resting precariously on my forked tongue
slithering and infusing that deep
sense of fear in the roots of your hair
as they stand at the back of your neck

I fear the day when my shredded truth
will drip and taint your soul
your pristine soul:
and your rambunctious gesture of owning everything
will crumble like a house of cards
in your phony wonderland

your ramshackle leash around my neck
hasn't choked me enough
to knock out the wind
out of my chest
those broken rods of resilience
though pounded a million times
with your sheer ignorance
hasn't given it yet

You,
with a smirk on your face
think I have caged my heart
but instead, I have given it an armor
a valiant shield,
against your vulture beak

as it tries fervently to preen the truth
from the depths of my soul
My bones rattle in a symphony
with crimson rage.
when men explain things to me.

Unappreciated

How can you live a life when the moments are
as long as the shrug of your shoulder?
or waiting on the careless fingers resting on a trigger
marked and unappreciated

How can you live life
when you are judged by your
cast/creed/skin color
or how your tongue moves inside you when you speak of love?

Those scriptures,
the world has forgotten—
while your knees are scraped blue
kneeling to pray to exalted Gods in heaven

How can you live life
when your desire and the rage of hormones
or the sex resting between your supple thighs,
marks and etches you?
and you can only rest in the binary form
any other is a direct violation of the life
soon to be dissolved;
should cease to exist.

How can you live life
like a broken spine of a book?
Still holding the old rotten pages together
with the essence,
soaked in between
the tattered pages—
but too old to be lifted off the shelves
thrown and resting
on an old broken armchair.

How can you live life like this?
Tell me, Can you?

Even My Grief Should Be Productive

Don't let the aroma leave the pickle jar
Keep the lid tight
my granny used to say—
Somethings are better left unspoken.
Part of your tradition
scream but not too loud.
Let the grief resonate with the insides of your skin.

We are picked and chosen precariously
through the callous thick fingers
Make sure they are not rotten...not stained enough
the flavor doesn't come through well.
I choose my memories
precariously, not the rotten ones
the shuddering truth
It should not shatter the patriarchy.

Let the anger morph.
Let it churn into the vermilion shade
the symbol of pride and ownership—
use your pain wisely
let them own you well

I used those broken whispers as a guide
to pluck the radishes out from the broken mud
of vegetable garden
moistened and broken by the summer rains
crumbled in pieces
but always rich in bounty

With bended knee scraping my soft skin.
I lowered myself whitened
by the heat of the summer sun
sweat and tears inseparable. A perfect concoction of pain.

A wicker basket filled to the brim
by the end of the day with the fruit of my labor
Grief pulled out from the dearth of acceptance.

A menagerie of suffocated desires
laid bare for your eyes
A lesson I have learned through the years
Even my grief should be productive.

An Exercise in Futility

Be ladylike,
eye-pleasing appearance
enough to gulp down the lies
down your swan bottled neck
oh! only to be bejeweled by the pearl necklace
and the bright possessions
he dons you with

Don't bother to breathe
when it's not ladylike
that your chest heaves violently
to the truth you fail to contain in
It's not social to use expletives in your
aristocratic language
you will be burned at the stake
for speaking your truth
your scraps will be fed to wolves

Don't wear your truth on your sleeves
which is naked and bold
it can't hold a gaze
with their shameful eyes
too hard to please;
too simple to ignore

Sit with your legs crossed
my mom used to say.
don't let that pointy opinions of your
evade your crisscrossed arms
to become an easy prey

Don't give them enough reasons
your piercing opinions
to point at your ribcage
they will choke you with
their blatant lies
will tear your heart apart
with their hungry eyes

Oh! look at him
he is remorseful

with his flagrant lies
he goes to church on Sundays
lives with his two daughters and his wife
that is enough for him to
seek the blessings of the male privilege
those damn vultures in disguise

Where the validity of your truth never mattered
it would never be
your reality will always
be a grain of sand in
their eyes of ignorance
too hard to ignore
too painful to acknowledge.
An exercise in futility.

resistance

I don't wait for you to corroborate my truth
evidence to prove the finality of my desires

I don't wait for your soft touches to smoothen my scars
a tourniquet to stop this bleeding

I don't want you to comfort me in the middle of the night
only to unravel my pain in the morning

as my body goes from a shade darker than yesterday
I don't need the assurance of the revolution around the corner

I birth my own revolution
and I create my own marches
the truth my soul owes to nobody but me

a conversation with my higher self
a divine ablution.
When I resist
I create.

Peace—A Metaphor for Denial

Peace, an act of ignorance
an act of denial is not a bliss   *no more*
when the silence is gutted like a fish
and the blood of your own fills the street.

How long can you be the puppet
in your own peaceful country?
the act of abandonment speaks a muted language
for all the hearts trapped like sparrows
on the other side of the town.

The wall creates a boundary between me   and humanity
they are still considered illegal with one foot in my land
another bloodied and stuck in the barbwire
that I put around God's own country.

I was born with a privilege
to call the piece of the earth my own
No matter it is laced and seeped
with someone's else blood
it belongs to me now

The young boy is shot
the pavement is colored by the shade of his blood
dark and useless;
to the people of this peaceful country

those who pull out the armrest and the beach chairs
to see the stars lit up the sky
and the deafening noise
muting the wails of a widowed mother.

They sip the beer as cold as their souls,
leaving the scene with a shrug and a short sigh.
Ignorance is bliss. Peace is a *metaphor* for *denial*
in this country, I call mine.

The Day the Town Celebrated

A stone thrown in a silent lake breaks its skin. Pain travels like ripples.
An outward fractal of grief continuously growing by every passing moment.

A single shot piercing through their soft bodies.
Piecing them with hate stringing the town.

Truth gaping through the open wound.
A lone gunfire shredding the sky into a million screams.

Only in this version love was not ostracized—
But burned and hanged in the Town square.

Hanged like pieces of meat for the devouring eyes circling them.
A prized possession for the cast that rules with an iron fist.

A mother runs half-naked through the empty street. Wailing.
Anger fracturing the thatched roofs.

Pain scratch like a pellicle dissolving in acid.
Its stench carried for generations.

Like folklore passed on from one babbling tongue to another.
How the little town's gazed gaping mouth like a blind cave

The time when love was not ostracized. Cast and Creed were thrown aside
when that small town gathered to celebrate the honor killing.

A Just Immigration Policy

Fear masquerading through
stone-cold heart and icy veins
diversity is a curse these days
a stain in the tapestry of the humanity

we are trying to lighten the fabric
they say,
less browning more white
it looks better in the night

the night when the moon turns ashen
crimson with the blood
running in sluice at the border walled-city
where the laughter is lost
but at least the chickens are "cage-free"

a body rejecting its own blood
sweat and the slime mixed together
bellies sucked in
you can count its ribs
a silhouette of my skeleton frame,
in the frothy moonlight
of your free country

where the water pitchers
are satiating the thirst of the
stones and the dirt trails
whitened by the summer sun
keeping the parched throats
still scratched and itchy

scarring the innards
of their marred skin
with their bony taloned fingers
trying to scrape
the stench of the refugee camps
out of their yellow skins

There is a method to your inhumanity
a perfect excuse,
an unapologetic application of
your *just* immigration policy.

Unforgivable

The rugged terrain of those unforgiving lanes
the ones warmed by the scorched feet
parched throats,
these blisters and welts have a story to tell
the suppurating skin begets mercy

Dreams glimmering in those bleary eyes
shimmering with the hopes of a foreign land
across the barbed wires:
whose pointy edges deemed softer
than the poking ends of AK-47 rifle on my naked throat

Dreams shattered—
my brown land turned into a deviant ocher shade
That rust,
the blood infested infection
devoured my childhood
slowly sucking away the sliver of air from my chest
a contagion unknown

My chest pounding in my heart.
ghosts of past resonating in the folds of my skin
The heart—
which still keeps the land of love neatly folded
like a pressed Dahlia. The faint strains of its fragrance
still, lace my dreams at night

Every turn and twist in the path
takes us nearer to the hope of finding a solace
in the land foreign to me.
Like a fly trapped in the window frame
feverishly,
I'm fleeing towards the lands of my salvation

Eyes bulging out, skin whitened by the summer sun
frail limbs, scorched backs
you can carve the silhouette of my bony frame
in your milky moonlight
I carry the prayers for your unborn child
prayers taught by grandmothers
in my pursed lips, a sacred hymn

You are the savior of my pulverized hopes
a sliver of a hope slowly withering,
But the dreams turn into a nightmare
seeing the air whizzing out of my newborn
a curse for a mother—
heaving chest burying the stench of death

How can you save the soul of a country?

A symbol of life, liberty, and pursuit of happiness
a country made from the colorful skin of millions
when you throw away the water: our sustenance
empties it on a dusty trail
in defiance of the love you once held.

Freedom, an Interpretation

What does freedom mean to
me, a dandelion?
as I continue my tryst with the
boastful wind
as it carries my identity on
it's fleeting wings

I tried with all my might
to hold onto my identity
but the cruel and the mighty winds
uprooted and carried me

I'm carried by my need
and desire to be rooted again
I'm an immigrant in my own
godforsaken land

I reach with all my failing might
with my bits severed
falling and rooting
clutching to the ground for its sustenance

See, I have to survive
this atrocity called war
a peaceful settlement
and rise through it
find a new patch of soil
call itself my home

dug my roots deeper to survive
the cold transformation,
of the ever-changing world

these boundaries and lines
don't make sense to me
when my identity has been dragged
and has been redefined
I end up getting the status of an
Immigrant.

The Day Liberty Was Disrobed

The serrated voices of the mottled fear
in those syllables
the smattering cacophony,
the syntax and semantics of unspoken fear
as if everything which makes sense around you
except for you:
except for the voices in your head.

We plead them to hear us once
just once,
before they carve out the pointy conviction
and chiseled them to suit their needs
to mold it back in the cookie-cutter hold
caulked by the hands of this unforgiving world

carving out the words from your tongue
which is free and unabashed
my rusted tongue unable to form words
You hold nothing more than a muted opinion
falling on the deaf ears standing on the curbside
stained by the blood of the unspoken and the untold

the collective conscious
living and breathing for generations
have lost their sanity
staying on the rim of the edge
of darkness and grim
a shade darker than
the limestone shade of death

How do you speak?
How do you voice your opinion anymore?
when the epitome of life liberty and pursuit of happiness
the one which stands by the Golden Door
has been scratched and engraved
a playground for graffiti carved by the immoral hands

to satiate the unending hunger
the Cerberus of wanting
those who hold the leash to freedom
are now guarding our speech and thoughts

refining the solemn words
written for centuries

those with their slithering tongues
and taloned fingers
are scraping and scratching
the last bits of life
from our solemn statue—
the epitome of liberty.

How to Be a Woman?

There are rules to be followed
guidelines to be remembered
regulations to be followed
to the T.

before I can call myself a woman
a lady like appearance—
an ever-present grin on my face
smiling from ear to ear,
just to ease you into the life
as you please.

I should bow down in obedience
should never raise my voice
walk with the stoop of discipline
and eat with your hand.
With the freedom, you have handed me on the plate
Like I was the chosen one, you see

Oh! that skirt is a little shorter than we expected
see it clearly fails to keep those lurking demon
inside their skin.
Now, you have shown them
too much flesh
now they will come out
will rip you into shreds
and devour your soul from within.

"*I told you*" they will say
keep your voice down
the patriarchy can't handle your pitch
they are tone-deaf to your songs of freedom
every war cry of yours
is not more than a mere screech

Give in to the fear of those jackals
those protectors lurking in the dark
they are the guardians,
the unabashed kings
of this society.

So next time the world tries to
teach me how to be a women
/an epitome of grace and elegance/
they should come and witness the scars
I bore on my body.

And the glow I carry
which can put their
thousand suns to shame
a sight their shameful eyes
can't bear to see.

Does Hurt Have a Gender?

What does a body want when it breaks down into
a million pieces? Its pulverized existence wanting acceptance.

Only to be ignored and walked over. Leftover like a day's old milk
on the kitchen counter. Forgotten and left to curdle.

Why do we keep numbing the sharp pain,
the knotted lamentation, caught in our hungry mouths?

Which cuts our souls both ways and leaves us to bleed in this world.
Profused with sweat and blood. A moment, indescribable.

Leaking and soaking the ridges of the curbside;
Here the thickness of your blood, its viscosity

And the gravitas of your speech depends on the color of your skin.
A pain, untenable.

An insurmountable pain rising in my mouth.
A dichotomy between pain and acceptance. A desire, abominable.

Does scream have a religion too? Do cries have a race?
Does hurt have a gender? Do wounds have a nationality?

Does your tongue curl into sin when you call out my name?
Does the triteness of the ideologies still mollify your pain?

True Lies

This lack of emergency
this hunger frothing between our teeth
we cuss and words are shredded
there can never be the truth
so pure and lies, so vile
which cannot be told these days

our ears are burned at the tips
truth is acidic some days
with eyes peeled in amazement
for the vile flooding the streets
and filling up the newspapers

those lies screaming
at the top of their tongues
and hounding at the
the right of the dial
those incessant pictures
running on the reels
like a hamster on the wheel

we gulp down
this atrocious so-called fake truth
and true lies
every damn day
and every single night

Hashtag Games

We play hashtag games
every time the evil scratches its belly
hunger plays on its forked tongue
mocking humanity.

A tag for every survivor
a label for everyday
smears the face with its ashen truth
justice delayed is justice denied
they willfully say.

A day to mourn the loss
where some girl regrets life
her dreams broken and pulverized
dying a muted death
the day changes
atrocity changes masks
a new hashtag and pain takes a new shape.

A New March,
a new route to follow
new placards to paint
new colors to wallow.

We keep strangulating our moments
life being squeezed out of it
Black Mondays and Dark Fridays
the debilitating pain;
till we find the new low and start all over again.

We play hashtag games
victims changes faces
a hamster on a wheel
but the perpetrator
remains the same.

Demarcation

That frail evening marking
the shadows of the long summer days
a bird perched on the barbed wires of the prison
demarcating happiness and the grief
acceptance and rejection,
solitude and the bouts of laughter,
the prisoner and the free

the arresting height of that boisterous wall
whose bricks are soaked
with the crackling wails and sobs
of the broken souls
neatly carved and plastered

a bizarre tinge of the ochre
peeling off from the walls
as the tears flow incessantly
through the bleary eyes as
they gaze from emptiness to nothing
silence culled in hollow bones
rattling with rage

palms holding out
for someone, something
for forgiveness,
a fleeting touch of humanity
a soft supple touch of love

a day wrapped around
the promises of second chances
silhouette of the loved ones
appearing between the thick bars
a pleasant sight for the cracked and pale eyes
death and silence are interchangeable

Go ask the bird?
as it sits at the barbed fence
keeping the two realms separate
a socially justifiable demarcation
between the cacophony and the melody
the symmetry and the dissonance

between the pristine and the ostracised

How thin is the separation between love and acceptance?
despair and the second chances,
between the judged and the forgiven.

Missed Boat

My home burnt down to ashes
walls painted with new shades of gore
a new shade of limestone and grey:
with fingers dipped in the blood
of my beautiful loved souls

My streets are laced
with death and macabre
the wailing cries of widows,
his lost son—with his broken bike
eating dust evermore

With dried-up trails on the face
eyes gazing from emptiness to nothing,
has painted a picture
of a new broken being

I'm digging hopelessly
with my bloody knuckles
looking for lost hope
in the pile of death and fear
trying to cover my back
with the last piece of
borrowed bread and tattered cloth

I'm trying to keep myself alive
knowing all the faces I have known
have been fed to the bloodhounds
in all its glory

I couldn't care less about
the orphaned kid next door
whose birth I celebrated
and danced till my feet went sore

All I care about now,
that I should run and hide
like a hunted prey
make sure not to miss the boat
which will take me
to the promised lands
far far away.

An Act of Self Defence

In memory of Ahmaud Arbery

The exact moment when the grief takes
shelter in your heart and leaves you undone
when the emptiness sits in the gaping hole
an abyss of loneliness:

the deafening lull in your mind stops making sense
the only loss which makes sense
are the lonely wails of the widow
in the apartment above you

Sorrow takes a different shape
when your tear starting pouring
for the senseless acts of violence and cowardice
carried by the very educated hands of this land
where life, liberty, and pursuit of happiness are
foundations of society, the sidewalks of those
are now pitted with the black bones of their own

You are not carrying your freedom in your arms
/your right to bear arms/
when the only right you have given to a mother
is to stick a cross in the middle of an unknown street
giving a piece of land for her dead son
when there is nothing but death at the end of a gun

When the names keep adding to the unnamed list
Treyvon, Michael, Eric....and so on
an ever-growing list of the dead and forgotten
where names have to scream out loud to
make their lives matter or else all hell will break loose

To hell with your right to the Second Amendment
when it's laced with the blood
of a black brother whose murder
you are incessantly
trying to justify as self-defense

Are You Listening, World?

I'm nowhere close to being a ball of anxiety
spooling continually in the close corridors of life
unraveling pain which has always been a secret task
a hushed affair:

the unbroken trails of tears have yet again
dusted by the ashes of dead and unknown
screaming from the headlines of the paper,
lying helpless at our doorsteps
waiting to be hauled in
we are averting our eyes to living these days

waiting for them to disappear in the dark cleavage of the night
that ashen night;
a witness of thousand incessant cries
a mother's wail is loudest than any noise you ever heard
Are you listening, World?
Are you listening, still?

when her womb has been scrubbed and scratched
with her hands tied in the back
when her heaving bosom has become
pools of salty tears
I scratch my pain
and see them growing in my scrawny veins
like the spider web—they are reaching everywhere

this uncontrolled growth of sadness
an ever-expanding pattern of grief
does it satiates your hunger for the freedom
when you lay lien to their soul
lay abandoned on the other side of the barb wires
their skin bearing the scratches of inhumanity

I wake every day taking a deep breath
inhaling the air laced with the tears of five years old
stripped away from love
an unmapped land carved around the gilded cage
his new home,
and exhaling my share of freedom
in a land built on the pursuit of life liberty and happiness.

My Body Is Nothing but a Sack of Blades

Pain moving like a fracture opening the crevasse.
A gaping wound.. An entry to the blind cave of my numb memories

The putrid smell of the burnished wounds scraped for time eternal
The wound loses the tourniquet to sullen time. Cuts and deepens.

Drips. Like blood in the water. Drips and stains. *Again.*

Anointing everything it touches. An outward growing fractal of pain.
Growing and overshadowing.

Night devouring everything with its black teeth. Tongue lolling,
slithering with desire. Sometimes touching a wound marks its existence.

My body is nothing but a sack of blades. An elegy for misplaced hope.

An open mouth of a blind well, where time loses its existence.
A dull blade. Every insult sharpening the edge a bit more.

Path to My Freedom

Walking precariously on the steep path
chosen by the boisterous men
tiptoeing between the serrated ends
Of misogyny and inequality.

With a whimper and a roar
I walk,
I run,
when the ground beneath my feet morphs and tumbles,
when every war of mine
is nothing but a mere screech to this tone-deaf patriarchy.

I laugh at the incredulity of pain
a tightrope strung between the dreams and reality,
Bowing down in obedience
walking with a stoop of discipline
With the freedom, you have handed me on the plate
like I was the chosen one, you see.

My head pointing towards the cerulean skies
laced with dreams and equality,
The pains of unspoken truths for generations
still lodged in my throat
I challenge my resolution
the fear to lose seeded deeply.

But I never give up—
As I learned from the footsteps of warriors
the path to my freedom is laced
with the blood of my determination
which their shameful eyes still can't bear to see.

My Survival Story

The slow cleaving in my backbone
the seamless transformation:
branching into my thousand selves
Like a sapling breaking
from the blind seed
I'm sprouting, I am thriving.

Growing like a Medusa
this fecundity of myself,
breaking out into
thousand versions of me
morphing into shapes
perfecting the art of topiary.

Like a reflection of the summer sun
shining into a million versions of me,
on shards of broken mirror
blessing them with its apricity.

I'm the war cry, the mortal fear
residing behind the enemy lines
The lava, the primordial gel
creating life so sublime,
I'm the knowledge in the verse
in the smattering cacophony of your mind.

With inked breaths and walnut skin
boisterous, unfettered, and uncontrolled,
Walking barefoot on this graveled path
unspooling life's fears in its intimate corridors.

My pain impaled on the stars in the nightly sky
I shine through my pulverized skin,
The broken pieces I foraged together
to make a whole of me
an untrammeled beauty within.

This fecundity is my survival extinct
to handle the plethora of emotions
life throws at me,
Undulating between the proximity and prosody of pain:
I'm learning. Yes, I'm growing.

My Body Lives like a Threat

A wound opens its mouth
and becomes self-inflicting
just like the night—
in its extreme
vulnerable to a ray of light
its existence challenged
and yet it stands bravely,
unfettered to the challenges of the dawn.

As I catch the words in my mouth
my language becomes an open threat
my razor speech falling sharp
on your dull convictions
we always exposed our deepest and softest part to heal
that's how the body learns
to heal;
to grow.

To be vulnerable is an elegy for acceptance.
We have hunger written all over us
with the ink as black as the mole
on your shoulder
challenging the frothiness of the moonlight.

my unspoken words sit like a welt
on my tongue in this foreign world
every time I twist my tongue
to shape a word,
I mispronounce your fear
a new threat is born.

Megha Sood is an Asian American Pushcart-nominated Poet, Editor, Author from Jersey City, New Jersey. An Associate Poetry Editor at journals *MookyChick* (UK), *Life and Legends* (USA), and Partner in Literary project "Life in Quarantine" with Stanford University, USA. Over 600+ Works featured including Poetry Society of New York, American Writers Review, Rising Phoenix Review, Kissing Dynamite, etc.

She is the recipient of the Poet Fellowship from Martha's Vineyard Institute of Creative Writing (MVICW) 2021, National Level Winner Spring Mahogany Lit Prize 2020, Three-Time State-level winner of NJ Poetry Contest. Second Place winner San Gabriel Valley Poetry Festival 2021, Finalist in Adelaide Literary Awards (2020), Poetry Super Highway (2020), Erbacce Prize (2020), TWIBB (2020), iWomanGlobalAwards (2020). Nominated "Author of the Year" by NY-based Spillwords Press.

Works selected numerous times by Jersey City Writers group, Jersey City Theater Center, and Department of Cultural Affairs for the Arts House Festival. Co-Edited anthologies (*The Medusa Project*, *MookyChick*) and ("The Kali Project, Indie Blu(e) Press). Poetry Judge for the SLAM Poetry competition, IITD Kaizen'21, and State level NAMI NJ Poetry Contest 2021. Panelist in WNBADC Chapter "Women in Poetry's Future". Performing venues includes New York Poetry Festival, Paterson Poetry Festival, Nuyorican Cafe, BrownStone Poets, OceanSide Library, Historic Apple Tree House, and many poetry festivals including "Anantha" by Samyukta Poetry, Jersey City Poetry Festival.

Author of forthcoming Chapbook (*My Body is Not an Apology*, Finishing Line Press, 2021) and Full Length (*My Body Lives Like a Threat*, FlowerSong Press, 2021). Blogs at https://meghasworldsite.wordpress.com/ and tweets at @meghasood16